Usborne
Sticker Dolly Dressing
Puppies & Kittens

Designed and illustrated by
Antonia Miller and Stella Baggott

Puppies

Written by Fiona Watt

Contents

A new puppy

Megan and Ellie are choosing their new puppy. They're watching the litter of puppies to see how they play with each other. They are looking for a puppy that's friendly, playful and curious.

Megan

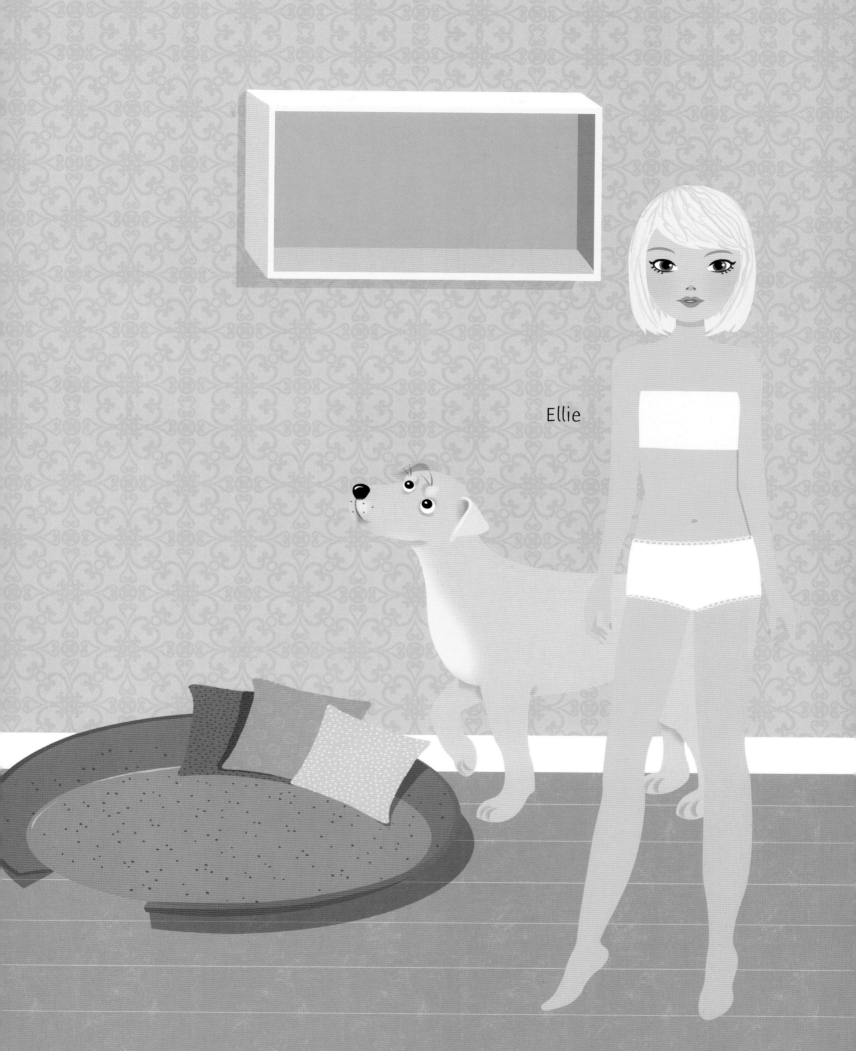

Ellie

Puppy party

It's Lauren's birthday and she's celebrating by meeting Elena and Alyssa in the park. Now that their puppies have been vaccinated, the dolls can walk them in the park and they can play with each other and meet other dogs.

Elena

Fern

Lauren

Buddy

Alyssa

Roxy

5

Dog boutique

Natalie and Lily are browsing the accessories, clothes and pampering products in a new boutique that has opened in town. Natalie's hoping to find a dog bowl for her puppy, Otto.

Lily

Otto

Natalie

Dog café

All dogs, puppies and their owners are welcome at the dog-friendly café, where they can relax and eat tasty treats. Even though Tilly doesn't have a dog of her own, she often goes to the café to meet dog-loving owners and their pets.

Tilly

Ruby

Alice

A walk in the woods

Olivia and Rosie are out walking Rosie's dog, Baxter. They've bumped into Izzy and her rescue dog, Lucky. The dogs are delighted to see each other and wag their tails wildly.

Rosie

Olivia

Baxter

Izzy

Training class

Sit... and stay! Mia, Lexie and Keira are learning how to train their dogs. Piper, Max and Coco already know to come when their names are called and now they are learning how to sit when they're told to.

Lexie

Mia

Max

Piper

Coco

Keira

Snowy walk

It snowed heavily last night, so Katya and Sophie are wrapped up in warm winter clothes. They've also put coats on their dogs to protect them from the icy wind.

Katya

Lola

Sophie

Daisy

Visiting the vet

Tanya has an appointment with the vet to have her puppy, Mitzy, microchipped. If Mitzy ever gets lost she can be scanned and Tanya's details will show up on the scanner.

Tanya

Jess

Alex

Ava

Polly

Playing in the park

Every morning the dolls meet with their dogs in the park. Molly, Kate's dog, loves to chase tennis balls, but Bracken is happy to stay close to Jade.

Molly

Asha

Jade

Kate

Bracken

Grooming salon

Ozzy's coat has been clipped and Jodie has washed him with a special dog shampoo that she's now rinsing away. Emma is trimming Belle's fur, but is styling it by leaving some parts longer than the rest.

Jodie

Ozzy

Emma

Belle

Dog show

This is the first year that Arianna, Holly and Freya have entered the annual dog show. The judges have awarded Cody 'Best in show'.

Arianna

Cody

Freya

Monty

Bonnie

Holly

Time for bed

Every night, Pepper the puppy curls up on the rug beside Millie's bed and falls asleep. He occasionally twitches and his paws quiver as he dreams of chasing squirrels.

A new puppy
Pages 2-3

Megan's outfit

Ellie's outfit

Puppy party
Pages 4-5

Elena's
leggings
and top

Lauren's top

Elena's dress

Alyssa's outfit

Elena's
shoes

Dog boutique
Pages 6-7

Natalie's outfit

Puppy outfits

Lily's outfit

Lily's puppy, Peanut

Dog café
Pages 8-9

Tilly's top

Alice's outfit
and apron

Tilly's outfit

Ruby's
top

Ruby's
dog,
Rocco

Rocco's
collar

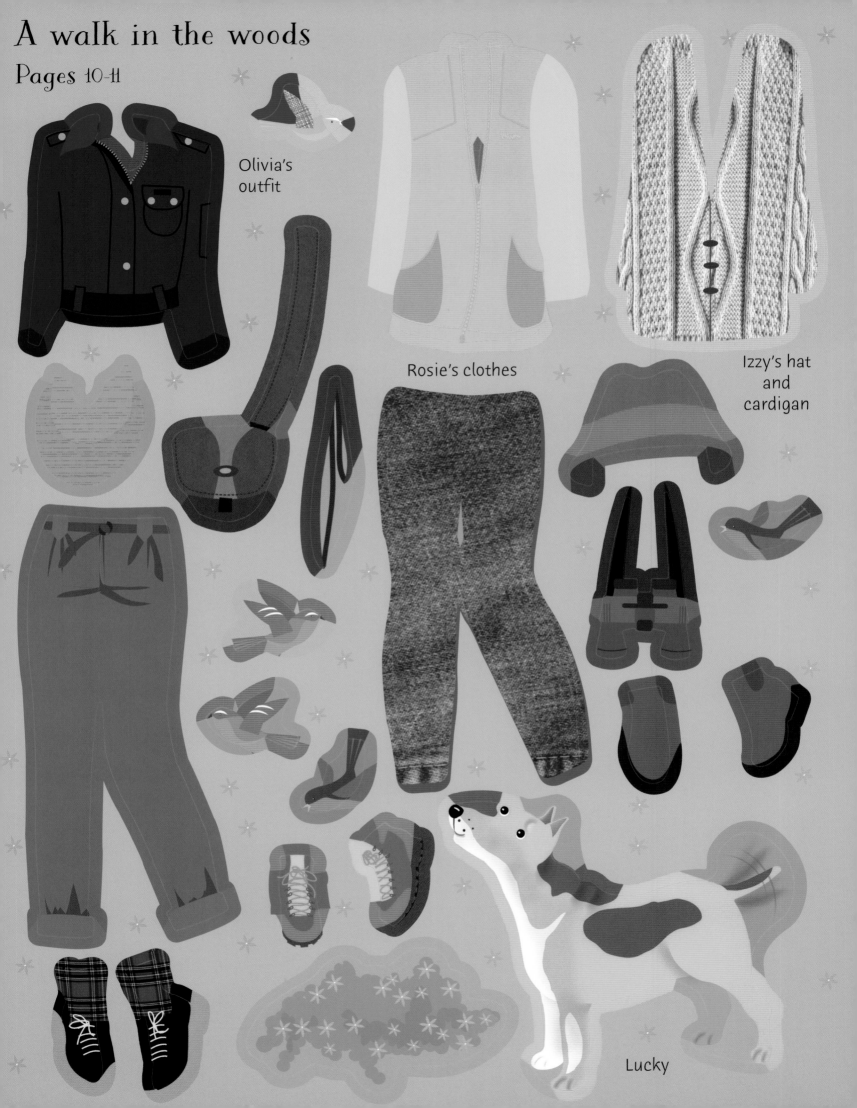

A walk in the woods

Pages 10-11

Olivia's outfit

Rosie's clothes

Izzy's hat and cardigan

Lucky

Training class
Pages 12-13

Keira's shoes

Keira's sweater

Lexie's top

Mia's cutoffs

Mia's sweater

Lola and Daisy's coats

Snowy walk
Pages 14-15

Sophie's hat

Sophie's outfit

Katya's jacket and boots

Visiting the vet
Pages 16-17

Tanya's outfit

Alex's top and pink shoes

Polly's outfit

Mitzy

Jess's top and boots

Playing in the park
Pages 18-19

Asha's outfit

Jade's top and scarf

Asha's coat

Jade's earmuffs

Kate's outfit

Asha's dog, Rex

Jodie's outfit

Emma's outfit

Jodie's shoes

Emma's top

Emma's boots

Dog show
Pages 22-23

Arianna's outfit

Holly's clothes

Freya's shirt

Time for bed
Page 24

Pepper

Usborne
Sticker Dolly Dressing
Kittens

Written by Lucy Bowman

Contents

A new cat

Three sisters have just adopted a cat. They decided to call him Snowball. They've prepared a room with everything he'll need to settle in – tasty food, fresh water, toys and a comfy bed. There are lots of new sights and smells, so they'll leave Snowball alone for a little while to explore.

Katie

Jess

Sophie

Hungry kittens

It's feeding time. Beth and Jade rattle boxes of food and their kittens come running. As a treat, each one gets a bowl of milk that's specially made just for kittens.

Beth

Jade

29

In the garden

These dolls are relaxing outside on a sunny afternoon, while their cats explore. There are butterflies to chase and blades of grass to chew. Scarlett is blowing pet-safe bubbles for the cats to catch and burst.

Alice

Ellie

Scarlett

Grooming

Sasha's cat, Leo, has a long furry coat that needs brushing to stay soft and healthy. Sasha has taken him to a cat salon, where Emma, the groomer will comb his fur with dry shampoo, clean his ears and eyes, and trim his claws. Leo loves the attention. Daisy and Marmaduke wait their turn.

Daisy

Sasha

Leo

Emma

Cat sitting

Layla, Chloe and Molly are looking after their friend's cats while she's away on a weekend trip. They've stopped by to give them fresh food, water and cuddles.

Layla

Chloe

Molly

Cat tower

Nicki and her friends have built a cat tower for their cats to climb.
It has lots for them to explore and enjoy – dangling toys to play with, houses
to hide in, a food bowl full of treats, and comfortable platforms to sleep on.

Nicki

Leah

Rashida

Visiting the vet

Daisy has taken her cat, Misty, to the vet for a check-up. She's been going to see Dr. Taylor since she was a kitten, so she isn't afraid. The waiting room is full of other cats waiting to be seen.

Amy

Caitlyn

Jo

Dr. Taylor

Daisy

Misty

Fostering

Lilly is fostering a cat called Calico – this means she will care for her until she finds a full-time owner. Calico had kittens a few weeks ago and now they're old enough to play and explore.

Grace

Lilly

Calico

Alex

Cat hotel

Jo, Naomi and Katya are going away for a few days, so they take their cats to stay at a cat hotel to be looked after. The cats' room has everything they need. They'll be well cared for with treats, games and cuddles.

Jo

Naomi

Katya

Party time

It's Megan's birthday and the dolls are hanging decorations for her party. Their kittens are excited by the boxes of streamers and ribbons, and want to play with them.

Megan

Aisha

Natalie

At the shelter

Riley and her friends are volunteering at an animal shelter, where stray cats live until they can be found new homes. Some of the cats are shy around people, so the dolls play with them to build their confidence. The more time the cats spend with the dolls, the safer they feel.

Riley

Charlotte

Zoe

Time for bed

Lucy and her two cats are getting ready for bed. She puts on her night clothes and says goodnight to Princess. Bobby has tired herself out playing all day and is already fast asleep.

Lucy

Princess

Bobby

A new cat
Pages 26-27

Katie's outfit

Sophie's clothes

Jess's outfit

Hungry kittens
Pages 28-29

Beth's clothes

Jade's outfit

In the garden
Pages 30-31

Alice's
hat

Ellie's top
and skirt

Ellie's shoes

Scarlett's outfit

Daisy's top

Marmaduke

Emma's clothes

Sasha's outfit

Cat sitting
Pages 32–35

Layla's skirt and top

Chloe's outfit

Molly's clothes

Molly's boots

Cat tower
Pages 36-37

Nicki's clothes

Rashida's top and skirt

Visiting the vet
Pages 38-39

Dr. Taylor's clothes

Leah's outfit

Jo's cat

Daisy's top

Amy's cat

Caitlyn's cat

Fostering
Pages 20-21

Lilly's clothes

Grace's outfit

Alex's clothes

Naomi's outfit

Katya's outfit

Jo's clothes

Party time
Pages 22-25

Aisha's top and skirt

Natalie's dress

Aisha's shoes

Megan's outfit

Natalie's boots

At the shelter
Pages 46-47

Charlotte's tops

Riley's outfit

Zoe's clothes

Time for bed
Page 48